CW01082686

Original title:
Through the Dream Door

Author: Thomas Sinclair
ISBN HARDBACK: 978-9916-90-822-8
ISBN PAPERBACK: 978-9916-90-823-5

The Puzzles of Enigmatic Nights

In shadows dance the whispers low,
Secrets wrapped in twilight's glow.
Stars blink softly, tales untold,
Mysteries in the night unfold.

Moonlight drapes a silver veil,
Casting dreams where echoes sail.
Footsteps follow paths unseen,
Lost in realms where none have been.

Each heartbeat syncs with whispered sighs,
As time weaves webs beneath the skies.
Stories linger, old yet new,
In every glance, a hidden clue.

With every star, a question gleams,
Filling silence with ancient dreams.
In the dark, the heart ignites,
Fighting shadows of enigmatic nights.

Ethereal Realities Awakened

In twilight's glow, the shadows dance,
Ghosts of dreams in a fleeting trance.
A world unveiled, in whispers take flight,
Awake, we drift in the soft moonlight.

Glimmers of hope through the veil arise,
Softly woven through starlit skies.
Each heartbeat pulses with magic untold,
In realms where the brave dare to be bold.

Mirage on the Edge of Wakefulness

Between the states of dream and thought,
Mirages flicker, fiercely sought.
Ephemeral visions start to blend,
As reality bends around each end.

The pulse of gold, the hue of night,
Flashes of joy, and flickers of fright.
On the cusp, where wishes take flight,
We chase our shadows into the light.

The Realm Where Wishes Whisper

In realms where wishes softly sigh,
Stars scribble secrets against the sky.
Each whisper born on a gentle breeze,
Invites the heart to find its ease.

Hope's melody plays a tender tune,
Under the gaze of a watchful moon.
In silence found beneath the stars,
Dreams take flight, transcending the scars.

Rift of the Imagination

A rift appears where thoughts collide,
Imaginations dance, and fears subside.
In painted hues, the worlds expand,
Each brush of fate by a steady hand.

The boundaries blur where we dare to dream,
Creating realms that shimmer and gleam.
In the tapestry of night, we unfurl,
A universe spun from a single swirl.

Night's Velvety Embrace

In shadows deep, where whispers play,
The stars ignite the velvet gray.
Moonlight drapes the silent trees,
Embracing night, a gentle breeze.

The world sleeps tight, a soft cocoon,
With dreams afloat beneath the moon.
Each heartbeat echoes, soft and slow,
In night's embrace, we drift and flow.

Wanderers in the Celestial Woods

Beneath the boughs of ancient dreams,
We wander through the silver beams.
The night is vast, our hearts alight,
As starlit paths unveil their sight.

Each step we take, the whispers call,
A symphony of nightfall's thrall.
With every breath, the cosmos sways,
In celestial woods, we lose our ways.

Embers of Dreams Entwined

Flickering flames of hopes once bright,
Dance within the soft twilight.
Embers spark in soft refrain,
As dreams entwine in sweet sustain.

Each flicker tells a tale of yore,
Of wishes cast from heart's core.
In warmth of night, they gently glow,
Guiding us where love can flow.

Beyond the Twilight Mirage

In the hush before the dawn,
Mirages weave, the night is drawn.
Phantoms of light in dance appear,
Beyond the twilight, visions near.

With every pulse, horizons shift,
The veil between dreams begins to lift.
In wonder lost, we find our gaze,
Beyond the mirage, time displays.

Mysterious Echoes in the Night

In the stillness, whispers call,
Beneath the moon, shadows fall.
Secrets dance on dusky air,
A haunting tune, sweet and rare.

Footsteps linger, faint and fleet,
Silhouettes in twilight meet.
Stars align, a cosmic sign,
Mysterious echoes intertwine.

Voices from the darkened past,
Through the ages, shadows cast.
Silent stories, softly spoken,
In the night, the silence broken.

Lost in dreams, all wanderers roam,
Through the dark, they seek a home.
In the echoes, find the light,
Mysterious whispers in the night.

Song of the Universe's Veil

In the silence, stars align,
A tender pulse, a cosmic sign.
Galaxies hum a gentle tune,
Draped in shadows of the moon.

Waves of stardust softly flow,
In the silence, secrets glow.
Between the worlds, the veils unfold,
Tales of mystery yet untold.

Harmony in every breath,
Life and death, a dance of death.
Through the universe's vast embrace,
We find our place, we find our grace.

Melodies of time and space,
In the silence, we find our place.
The universe sings through night,
In every heart, a spark of light.

Whispers Beyond the Veil

Beyond the veil, a soft refrain,
Echoes linger, joy and pain.
In the twilight, where shadows blend,
Whispers rise, our souls to mend.

Fragments of a hidden song,
Carried by the winds along.
In the stillness, we take flight,
Whispers dancing in the night.

Voices call from realms unknown,
In their warmth, we find our home.
Through the mist, we seek and find,
Whispers weaving, intertwined.

Light and shadow, forever cast,
In the echoes, stories past.
Whispers guide us, soft and pale,
Leading us beyond the veil.

Shadows in the Gossamer Light

In the twilight, shadows creep,
Secrets buried, dreams we keep.
Gossamer threads, they weave and twine,
In the light, the shadows shine.

Beneath the stars, our hopes do soar,
In the silence, we yearn for more.
Whispers linger, soft and bright,
Shadows dance in gossamer light.

Softly glimmering like a dream,
Echoes flow like a silver stream.
In the darkness, find our spark,
Shadows glowing in the dark.

Through the night, the stories wend,
Paths entwined that never end.
In each shadow, find delight,
Dancing softly in the light.

The Light Beyond the Dreamscape

In shadows where the whispers play,
The light begins to gently sway,
Through silent paths where dreams entwine,
A glimmer glows, so soft, divine.

With every breath, the vision stirs,
Awakening the heart's sweet purrs,
Carving truths from night's embrace,
In this realm, we find our place.

Beyond the haze, the dawn will break,
A world remade, for hope's own sake,
Infinite skies, bright and wide,
In every dawn, our souls abide.

Awaking the Silent Stories

In quiet corners, echoes found,
The tales of yore weave 'round and 'round,
Each silent story holds a key,
Unlocking dreams, setting them free.

Whispers linger, soft and low,
In hearts of those who seek to know,
With every turn of faded page,
Awakens worlds, ignites the sage.

Witness the past in shadows gleam,
As memory drifts, a flowing stream,
Each word a brush, each line a hue,
Painting lives, both old and new.

Bridges of Light and Memory

Across the chasm, a path we weave,
With threads of gold, we dare believe,
In every step, a spark ignites,
Building dreams on starry nights.

Bridges form between the hearts,
Connecting worlds where safety starts,
In laughter shared and tears that fall,
In the light, we find our call.

With every pulse, our stories grow,
In unity, we learn to flow,
Together strong, we face the tide,
On bridges built with love as guide.

Secrets of the Sable Night

Night unfolds with secrets shy,
Beneath its veil, the shadows lie,
In velvet darkness, dreams ignite,
Whispers beckon, silent flight.

Stars are lighthouses, distant bright,
Guiding souls through sable night,
In hidden corners, tales unwind,
Fables born of a tender mind.

Each starlit whisper, a treasure mild,
Secrets cradled, softly filed,
In the hush of dreams, we rise,
To greet the dawn through quiet sighs.

The Bridge to Ethereal Reveries

Upon a misty bridge I stand,
Gazing at shimmering strands,
Woven of light and whispers soft,
Carrying dreams, aloft and waft.

The stars above, they gently gleam,
Guiding the pathways of my dream,
Each step reveals a tale untold,
Where secrets of the heart unfold.

Through twilight hues, the echoes dance,
Inviting souls to take a chance,
With every note, a story grows,
On this bridge that softly glows.

Ethereal winds caress my face,
In this serene and sacred space,
Where time dissolves, and thoughts take flight,
On the bridge to realms of light.

Nestled in Seraphic Dreams

In fields of gold where shadows play,
Seraphic visions guide the way,
Soft petals fall from skies above,
Enfolding hearts in gentle love.

A lullaby the breezes sing,
As starlit whispers gently cling,
Nestled in dreams, we drift and sway,
Where night transforms the light of day.

The moonlit glow illuminates,
Each corner where enchantment waits,
Wrapped around in silken threads,
Where hope and joy, like rivers, spread.

Awakening to morning's grace,
The dreams still linger in their place,
In memories of twilight's scheme,
Forever held in seraphic dreams.

Fables of the Starlit Corridor

In the corridor where starlight weaves,
Fables dance on gossamer leaves,
Each shimmer whispers tales of yore,
Echoed softly, forevermore.

With every step, the legends call,
In shadows deep, we rise and fall,
On pathways paved with cosmic dust,
In starlit tales, we place our trust.

The night reveals our dreams' desire,
Igniting hearts with ancient fire,
Where time and space do intertwine,
In fables spun of the divine.

Beyond the veil where secrets dwell,
Each story lingers like a spell,
In this corridor, we explore,
The endless wonders we adore.

The Threshold of Imagination

At the threshold where thoughts ignite,
Imagination takes its flight,
With colors bright and visions clear,
Creating worlds that draw us near.

Beyond the door, the wonders bloom,
Casting away all doubt and gloom,
A canvas stretched across the skies,
Where every dream is born to rise.

We wander through the realms of light,
In every corner, pure delight,
Crafting stories, bold and free,
Embracing all that we can see.

As laughter echoes, hearts expand,
In this enchanted, timeless land,
Each step we take, a spark divine,
At the threshold, all is mine.

Journeys Within the Fabric of Night

In shadows deep, where silence dwells,
The stars weave tales, as the night swells.
Cloaked in dreams, we drift and roam,
Within the fabric, we find our home.

Echoes whisper through the dark,
Guiding souls, igniting spark.
Footsteps light on paths unknown,
Each heartbeat stirs, a world grown.

Veils of mystery cradled tight,
Stars above, we chase the light.
In the vastness, we lose our fears,
Each journey deepens through the years.

And as dawn starts to break the night,
We carry dreams into the light.
In every shadow, echoes sing,
Our journeys vast, on night's sly wing.

Glimmers in the Twilight Mist

Softly falls the twilight mist,
Secrets hidden, a gentle kiss.
Glimmers dance on water's edge,
Nature whispers, a sacred pledge.

In valleys low, and mountains high,
Colors blend beneath the sky.
Fleeting moments, time stands still,
In twilight's glow, we find our thrill.

Memories weave through the soft breeze,
Carrying dreams with effortless ease.
With every step, the world awakes,
In twilight glow, no more mistakes.

The night will come to seal the fate,
But in this space, we contemplate.
Glimmers shine, like stars so far,
Illuminating who we are.

Secrets Bloom in the Dreamscape

In the hush of night, secrets bloom,
Among the stars, casting their gloom.
A tapestry stitched by silken thread,
In whispered dreams, all fears have fled.

Awakened minds drift and sail,
Through nebulae, we leave a trail.
Each thought a petal, soft and bright,
In the garden of the endless night.

Visions stir in colors bold,
Stories of the young and old.
Glimmers of truth, hidden yet near,
Each secret shared, a cherished cheer.

Within this space, the heart takes flight,
In the vast expanse, all feels right.
Each dream unfolds a new embrace,
In the dreamscape's warm, endless grace.

Beyond the Horizon of Sleep

Beyond the horizon, dreams take flight,
Where the stars twinkle against the night.
In slumber's grasp, we wander far,
Guided gently by the evening star.

Mysteries beckon, shadows play,
In the quiet realms where whispers sway.
With every breath, the night unveils,
A world where wonder never fails.

Softly drifting through the veil,
Magic beckons, we cannot fail.
In twilight realms, hope springs anew,
As hearts ignite with every view.

Awake we rise, with shadows shed,
Carrying dreams like threads unsaid.
Beyond the horizon, we shall leap,
Embracing all we find in sleep.

Shimmering Gateways to the Unknown

Beyond the veil where shadows play,
Bright whispers call, beckoning sway.
Stars alight in endless flight,
Guide us through the veil of night.

Each step we take, a mystery unfolds,
Secrets in the twilight, gently told.
Doors of silver, paths of gold,
Into the realm where dreams are bold.

The air is thick with unspent dreams,
Floating softly on starlit beams.
Through shimmering gates, we drift and roam,
Finding heartbeats that feel like home.

In shadows deep, our spirits rise,
Transcending all the earthly sighs.
Endless wonders await our quest,
In the unknown, we find our rest.

The Voyage Beyond Sleep's Abyss

In whispers sewn with evening's thread,
We sail beyond where dreams are fed.
A sea of stars, vast and wide,
Embraces souls on the night's tide.

Every wave sings lullabies sweet,
As we drift softly, hearts in beat.
Lost in the depths, where shadows dwell,
We find the tales that night will tell.

Fog drapes like velvet, cool and light,
Drawing us deeper into the night.
Through realms of whimsy, we shall glide,
On silvery sails, where fears abide.

The voyage calls from the edge of dreams,
Where nothing's ever as it seems.
With open hearts, we brave the deep,
In the abyss, we learn to leap.

Fragments of Night's Embrace

In night's embrace, the fragments glow,
Flickering softly, weaving slow.
Memory dances on shadows cast,
Whispers of stories long since passed.

Stars tumble down like scattered mirth,
Filling the void with their soft birth.
A tapestry of silence hums,
Drawing us close to where it comes.

Each fragment holds a tale of yore,
Echoes of laughter, shadows that soar.
In twilight's grasp, we gather light,
Holding the pieces of endless night.

Cloaked in mystery, the night bestows,
The warmth of dreams that gently glows.
In fragments found, we are made whole,
Through night's embrace, we touch the soul.

Labyrinth of the Lullaby

In the labyrinth where echoes play,
Soft lullabies weave night and day.
Through winding paths that whisper low,
Secrets of dreams that gently flow.

A lantern glows in the misty haze,
Guiding lost hearts through winding ways.
In quiet corners, shadows dance,
Inviting the soul to take a chance.

Twilight gathers in cradled light,
Embracing the dreamers of the night.
With every turn, a new surprise,
In the lullaby, the heart flies.

Through twisted lanes and paths unseen,
We wander where the night is keen.
In this maze of tender song,
We find the place where we belong.

The Lure of the Lost Stars

Whispers of light from afar,
Guide the seekers with dreams bizarre.
In twilight's embrace, they softly gleam,
Fading hopes entwined in a celestial dream.

Sprinkles of fire in the ocean of night,
Holding the stories of forgotten flight.
Each twinkle a promise, a wish in the dark,
A map of the heart, igniting a spark.

Beneath the vast sky, a longing unfolds,
The lure of lost stars, a mystery bold.
With every glance, they beckon us near,
Carrying tales of love and sheer fear.

When dawn chases shadows and bids them goodbye,
The whispers of starlight still flicker and sigh.
In silence, we ponder the paths that were crossed,
Forever enchanted by what we have lost.

Chasing Shadows of Forgotten Tales

In the corners of memory, shadows reside,
Stories buried, where dreams once abide.
Fragments of laughter, whispers of woe,
Chasing the shadows, where none dare to go.

Through the echoes of time, we wander and seek,
A tapestry woven with threads worn and weak.
Each shadow a whisper, a story retold,
Of heroes and lovers, of brave hearts so bold.

As twilight descends, the shadows elongate,
In silence we gather the tales that await.
For every lost moment, a new one will rise,
Chasing the shadows beneath endless skies.

So let us remember, let us not fade,
The tales of the past, in our hearts they cascade.
With ink and with passion, let stories ignite,
Chasing shadows, we bring forth the light.

Symphony of the Dream Weaver

Softly the moon spins a silken thread,
Weaving our dreams while we rest our heads.
Each note a whisper, a sigh of the night,
A symphony hidden, yet burning so bright.

With colors of twilight, the fabric unfolds,
Stories of mystics and secrets untold.
In harmony's embrace, we soar and we glide,
Carried by visions on the silvery tide.

The weaver of dreams plays a delicate hand,
Crafting our hopes in this soft, gentle land.
Each heartbeat a rhythm, a dance in the dark,
As shadows perform to the glow of a spark.

Awake once again, our spirits take flight,
Bathed in the warmth of a new morning light.
With whispers of wonder, we find what we seek,
In the symphony woven, our souls gently speak.

Within the Threads of Images

Captured in stillness, a moment reveals,
The stories we treasure, the truth that heals.
Within the threads of images spun,
Lives intertwine, and journeys begun.

Colors and textures dance in the frame,
Each photo a heartbeat, a flicker of flame.
Frozen in time, yet alive in our hearts,
Every glance taken, a piece of the arts.

Through laughter and sorrow, we gather our past,
A gallery built on shadows that cast.
In the tapestry formed, we find our own way,
Within the threads of images, memories stay.

So let us look closely, let us not forget,
The beauty in moments, in kindness, in debt.
We are but images, connected in space,
Within the threads of life, we find our grace.

Veils of Enchantment Awakened

In twilight's grasp, the shadows play,
Soft whispers call, as colors sway.
With every breath, a magic spun,
Awakened dreams, the night begun.

Through silvered mists, the moonlight drifts,
Casting awake the heart's soft lifts.
Each thread of starlight, a tale of old,
Veils in the dark, enchantments unfold.

The forest hums, a gentle tune,
Beneath the gaze of the watching moon.
In secret glades, where fantasies bloom,
Veils of wonder, dispelling gloom.

Awaken, oh heart, to realms anew,
In shadows deep, where magic grew.
The night is ripe, with dreams to share,
Veils of enchantment, light as air.

Dances of the Luminous Thought

In realms where ideas begin to glide,
Thoughts intertwine, a radiant tide.
Dancing shadows, flickering bright,
Luminous whispers in the velvet night.

Each moment spins, a vivid hue,
Coloring realms both fresh and true.
Ideas swirl like leaves in flight,
Dances of the luminous thought, delight.

With every pulse, new visions bloom,
As dreams emerge from silence's loom.
A tapestry spun from night's soft grace,
Carried in hearts, no time can erase.

Questions linger, like stars unchained,
In the quiet corners, wisdom gained.
Every thought a journey sought,
In dances of the luminous thought.

The Realm Where Night Whispers

In twilight's hush, the world takes pause,
To listen close, to night's soft laws.
Each star a secret, each breeze a song,
In shadows deep, where dreams belong.

The moon's gentle sigh, a tender thread,
Weaving stories in silence spread.
Where echoes blend with the softest sighs,
The realm where night whispers never dies.

Beneath the veil of the inky sky,
Thoughts take wing, on dreams they fly.
In velvet tones, the cosmos speaks,
In quiet moments, the heart seeks.

A tapestry spun of whispers rare,
In stillness found, where souls lay bare.
The night unfolds its soft embrace,
In the realm where night whispers grace.

Portals Cast in Asleep's Embrace

In slumbered realms, the portals gleam,
Where echoes of reality weave a dream.
Every sigh a bridge to what could be,
Portals cast in asleep's embrace, set free.

Through softened light, where shadows blend,
Dreams unfurl, a lover's friend.
In fleeting moments, time stands still,
As magic whispers, our hearts to thrill.

The night's caress, an endless flight,
In dreams we wander, lost in the night.
With every heartbeat, we drift away,
In portals cast, where wishes play.

Awake or asleep, the worlds collide,
In slumber's hold, we gently glide.
Through realms unseen, our spirits trace,
Portals cast in asleep's embrace.

Nocturnal Journeys and Silent Stars

Beneath a veil of whispered night,
Moonbeams dance with silver light.
Shadows twist in secret dreams,
Echoes of forgotten themes.

Winding paths through starlit skies,
Where the gentle darkness lies.
Every twinkle holds a tale,
Of the brave who dared to sail.

Footsteps soft on ancient ground,
In the quiet, solace found.
Wondrous worlds await afar,
Guided by a silken star.

As the night unfolds its grace,
Time transcends in this embrace.
Onward through the cosmic seas,
We become what we believe.

Fantastical Fables at Daybreak

In the blush of morning's light,
Whispers weave through dreams of night.
Creatures born from tales of yore,
Awake to greet a fabled shore.

Cascading laughter fills the air,
Magic swells with bright affair.
Colors bloom like flowers rare,
Painting stories everywhere.

Every shadow casts a spell,
Secrets kept, yet hard to quell.
In the hearth of noon's warm glow,
Fantastical tales start to flow.

Chasing echoes of the past,
Adventures made to ever last.
In the heart where myths reside,
The truth and wonder coincide.

Pathways of the Waking Imagination

Close your eyes, take a deep breath,
Step into the world of depth.
Paths that twist and turn anew,
Unveil the dreams that call to you.

In the garden of your thought,
Every moment, deeply sought.
Rivers flow where wishes gleam,
Casting forth a vibrant dream.

Painted skies with stars so bright,
Guide the steps in morning light.
Footprints left on shifting sands,
Narrate tales from distant lands.

Awake to find the dreams reside,
Within your heart, your truest guide.
Every thought a vivid spark,
In the pathways, roam and mark.

The Alchemy of Lucid Visions

In the realm where visions blend,
Thoughts transform and never end.
Gold and silver spun with care,
Crafted dreams float in the air.

Lucid whispers, softly flow,
Through the heart where secrets glow.
Alchemy of night and day,
Turns the ordinary to sway.

Moments captured in a glance,
Lead the soul to daring chance.
Sketches of the yet unseen,
Map the wonder where we've been.

Let desires guide your way,
Through the twilight into play.
With each thought a magic key,
Unlock the doors of what can be.

Luminescent Shadows at Play

In twilight's grasp, they softly glide,
Ghostly forms in twilight's tide.
With whispers low, they weave and sway,
Luminescent shadows at play.

Beneath the trees, where secrets dwell,
Stories spin in a distant spell.
Flickering lights in a mystic fray,
Dance with the night, in shadows, they play.

A flicker glows, then fades away,
As dreams entwined begin to stray.
These fleeting glimpses, bright and gay,
Remind us all of night's ballet.

Whirling memories in gentle light,
Echoes holding the whispers tight.
In every gust, in every sway,
Luminescent shadows at play.

Windows to the Unconscious

Eyes mirror depths we barely know,
Veils of thought in silent flow.
Glimmers of truth that gently show,
Windows to the unconscious aglow.

Dreams unfolding like petals rare,
Fragments of moments suspended in air.
In stillness found, seekers dare,
To peer through glass, to moments bare.

Questions linger like shadows cast,
Stories etched in the fabric of past.
We search for meanings that ever last,
Through windows to the unconscious, vast.

Whispers of souls that once did dwell,
Echoing secrets our hearts compel.
In darkened corners where thoughts excel,
Lie windows to the conscious, a spell.

Bearing Witness to the Unseen

In silence deep, we linger still,
Bearing witness to the unseen thrill.
The gentle touch of a hidden will,
A world alive, a boundless quill.

Echoes sing through the empty air,
Unfolding truths that few will share.
Moments entwine without compare,
Bearing witness, with mindful care.

What glimmers bright beyond the sight,
Holds hidden stories of day and night.
In shadows deep, they take their flight,
Bearing witness to the unseen light.

A heartbeat's pulse, a sigh's embrace,
Through silence, we find our rightful place.
In every corner, in every space,
We bear witness to time's gentle grace.

Dances of Light Beneath Stars

In the quiet night, we take our stand,
Dancing light on a silver strand.
Beneath the stars, dreams expand,
Dances of light, a cosmic band.

Whispers of winds in the midnight air,
Twinkling bright with a celestial flare.
Footsteps trace a path so rare,
Dances of light beyond compare.

Galaxy's breath in gentle sway,
Guides us through the night's ballet.
In stardust trails, we find our way,
Dances of light, the night's bouquet.

Embers rise from every heart,
In music's hold, we play our part.
Under the stars, as dreamers start,
Dances of light, pure works of art.

Beyond the Cloak of Slumber

In shadows deep, the whispers sigh,
The moonlight dances, a lullaby.
Softly we drift on the velvet night,
Where dreams take shape, and fears take flight.

A world unfolds with each gentle breath,
A realm of wonders, beyond all death.
Stars weave tales in the silent air,
In slumber's grip, we're free from care.

Echoes of laughter, a fleeting sound,
Through twilight paths, our hearts are unbound.
Time loses meaning in this embrace,
In the cloak of slumber, we find our place.

As dawn approaches, the visions fade,
Yet in our hearts, the dreams have stayed.
With open eyes, we greet the day,
Beyond the cloak, we find our way.

Adventures in the Fabric of Dreams

Threads of wonder weave through the night,
Adventures unfold in whispered flight.
Each tapestry glimmers with tales untold,
In the fabric of dreams, our spirits bold.

We sail on clouds, through skies of fire,
Chasing the echoes of wild desire.
Every journey born from a restless heart,
In this realm, we create our art.

With each stitch, a new story begins,
A dance with shadows, where magic spins.
Mountains rise and oceans gleam,
In the heart of the night, we dare to dream.

So when morning breaks and dreams take flight,
Remember the magic that glows in the night.
For in every heartbeat, adventure gleams,
Alive in the fabric, the essence of dreams.

Beneath the Canopy of Wishes

Beneath the stars, our secrets twine,
In the silver glow, our hopes align.
Dreams like fireflies light the night,
A canopy woven in gentle light.

We whisper softly to the moon above,
Each wish a promise, each heart a dove.
With every breath, the universe spins,
In the canopy where magic begins.

Time stands still as we cast our fate,
In this sacred space, we patiently wait.
The night, a canvas for our desires,
Beneath the sky, our hearts catch fire.

As dawn approaches, wishes take wing,
Carried on breezes with the joy they bring.
With faith anew, we embrace the day,
Beneath the canopy, we find our way.

Colors of the Midnight Mirage

In the silence of night, colors collide,
A mirage dances where shadows hide.
Crimson and azure swirl in the dark,
Drawing us close to that luminous spark.

Silken hues wrap around our dreams,
Painting the sky with glittering beams.
Emerald whispers and gold-tipped sighs,
In the heart of the night, where magic lies.

Through the cockpit of stars, we soar on high,
Chasing reflections that flicker and fly.
Each color a heartbeat, each shade a song,
In the midnight mirage, we all belong.

So let us wander, let visions ignite,
In this world where dreams meet twilight.
For in colors bright, we'll always find,
The essence of wonder, forever entwined.

Treading the Path of Slumbering Souls

In shadows deep where whispers dwell,
The echoes of the night do swell.
With every step, the silence shares,
The secrets held by dreamers' lairs.

Beneath the veil of starlit skies,
Where time and space commence to rise.
We wander through this tranquil grace,
Exploring realms of time and space.

The quiet breath of night's embrace,
Invites us to a softer place.
Among the dreams we're drawn to find,
The patterns of the sleeping mind.

Through winding paths of softest light,
We tread the dreams that weave the night.
On slumber's wings, our spirits soar,
In realms of peace forevermore.

Flickers from the Unseen

In twilight's grasp, the shadows play,
Where childhood fears and hopes lay.
The flickers dance in muted hues,
Revealing truths we seldom choose.

Between the worlds, they gently glide,
With whispers of the dreams we've tried.
To grasp the light that ebbs and flows,
In corners where the darkness grows.

Yet sparkles stream from unseen realms,
And guide the heart that boldly helms.
In every flicker, we may sense,
The beauty found in past defense.

So reach beyond what eyes can see,
Embrace the flickers, wild and free.
For in the shadows, light will bloom,
And banish fears that leave a gloom.

Parables of the Midnight Realm

In midnight's hour, the stories weave,
With threads of dreams that hearts believe.
The parables unfold with grace,
In this enchanted, hidden space.

Each fable speaks of loss and gain,
Of joys that gleam and sift through pain.
The shadows cloak the lessons learned,
In every twist, the fate is turned.

The owls confer with ancient lore,
While starlight hints at something more.
Through whispered tales, we find our way,
In lessons taught by night and day.

Embrace the magic, let it flow,
The midnight realm holds treasures low.
In every parable's embrace,
We find our truth, our sacred space.

The Enigma of Drowsy Spheres

There lies a mystery in the night,
In drowsy spheres where dreams take flight.
Each orb a chance for eyes to close,
And wander where the silence grows.

Like whispers caught in twilight's sheen,
The drowsy spheres, both strange and keen.
They beckon with a soft allure,
To explore the depths, both dark and pure.

In every turn, a riddle found,
The worlds beyond, both lost and bound.
In slumbered thoughts where mysteries bloom,
We trace the lines where shadows loom.

So float within this gentle sway,
Let drowsy spheres lead you away.
For in the depths of sleep's embrace,
We find our dreams in time and space.

Passageways of Chimerical Light

In twilight's grasp, the whispers call,
Through veils of mist, where shadows fall.
A dance of dreams, the spirits play,
In passageways, they find their way.

Amidst the glimmer, visions bloom,
In fleeting echoes, they dispel gloom.
Chimerical realms, where hopes take flight,
We wander lost in ethereal light.

With every step, a story told,
In colors bright, in hues of gold.
These winding paths, so rich and rare,
Lead to a world beyond compare.

So let us roam where few have been,
Through passageways of ever-seen.
For in each turn, a wonder lies,
In chimerical light, our spirits rise.

Secrets of the Midnight Portal

In silence deep, the stars align,
A portal glows, a thread divine.
Secrets whisper, the night unfolds,
A tale of dreams, of legends told.

Through shadows deep, the passage sways,
A beckoning light, through tangled ways.
Within the dark, the magic brews,
In midnight's shroud, we dare to choose.

Each heartbeat echoes, time stands still,
The essence of fate is ours to fill.
Secrets hidden in velvet skies,
In midnight's grasp, our hope complies.

So step on through, embrace the unknown,
For in this world, we are not alone.
The midnight portal calls us near,
To secrets lost, in whispers clear.

Shadows in the Realm of Reverie

In dreams we tread, on whispers light,
In shadows cast, we dance with night.
The realm unfolds, a misty sea,
Of endless thoughts, of what could be.

Each fleeting glance, a masterpiece,
In reverie's hold, we find our peace.
A tapestry of hopes and fears,
In shadowed grace, we shed our tears.

With every breath, the echoes swell,
In this soft realm, where spirits dwell.
A dance of souls, in twilight's breath,
In shadows deep, we conquer death.

So linger on, in this sweet haze,
Where time stands still, in a tender gaze.
For in this realm, we are set free,
To wander on in reverie's spree.

Dance of the Lunar Key

When silver moonbeams touch the ground,
A lunar key spins 'round and 'round.
Unlocking dreams with every sway,
In night's embrace, we find our way.

A dance of shadows, soft and light,
Guiding hearts through endless night.
With each twirl, the world takes flight,
In harmony with the stars so bright.

The whispers of the night reveal,
Secrets hidden, we can feel.
With every step, we are entwined,
In the dance of fate, our souls aligned.

So let us waltz where dreams reside,
In moonlit realms, where love won't hide.
For in this dance, we find our key,
To worlds unknown, in unity.

Enigmas in the Land of Dreams

In shadows deep where whispers dwell,
The secrets weave a mystic spell.
With moonlit paths that twist and turn,
Awake the thoughts we yearn to learn.

Through velvet skies of swirling night,
The stars hold tales that dance in flight.
Each dream a door, a portal wide,
In slumber's arms, we drift and glide.

Voices echo in the breeze,
Calling forth the lost and free.
In silence, seek what remains unseen,
The truth hidden, serene and keen.

So wander forth, embrace the haze,
In this land where time decays.
Enigmas wait in every stream,
Unlock your heart, and live the dream.

Celestial Crossroads of the Mind

At twilight's brink, the thoughts align,
Where pathways cross, your fates entwine.
Each choice a star, so brightly spun,
Igniting paths where dreams are won.

In silence hums the cosmic tune,
A melody beneath the moon.
The mind's vast skies, a canvas wide,
Where hopes and questions coincide.

A flicker here, a spark of light,
Illuminates the endless night.
With every thought, a universe,
In whispers soft, you will traverse.

So take a breath, and hold on tight,
At crossroads vast, find your true sight.
Celestial wonders gently guide,
In realms of thought, let truth abide.

The Dimensional Drift

In realms where boundaries intertwine,
The drift awaits with secrets fine.
Step through the veil, embrace the flow,
To worlds unknown where dreams can grow.

Each flicker bends the time and space,
An odyssey with endless grace.
Beyond the stars, the colors blend,
A tapestry that has no end.

In the silence, echoes call,
Of timeless whispers, rise and fall.
Through shifting sands of what may be,
Find fragments of your memory.

So journey forth, give in to fate,
In every shift, open the gate.
The dimensional drift awaits your heart,
Where every start is a brand new art.

Gossamer Threads of Fantasia

On gossamer threads that softly spin,
The visions travel, lose and win.
A dreamscape woven with such care,
In hues of magic, light as air.

Each thread a tale of joy or woe,
A dance of colors, bright and slow.
As faeries whisper to the trees,
The heart finds peace upon the breeze.

Through wondrous lands of make-believe,
Where every glance, the soul can weave.
In softness lies the power found,
In every beat, your dreams are crowned.

So let your spirit take to flight,
In fantasy's embrace, find the light.
Gossamer threads will guide your way,
Through realms unseen, where heart can play.

Twilight's Palette on the Canvas of Night

Colors blend as day takes flight,
Whispers fade into the night.
Stars awaken, soft and bright,
Painting dreams in silver light.

Shadows dance on gentle streams,
Merging softly with our dreams.
Crickets sing their soothing themes,
In twilight's hush, the heart redeems.

Clouds drift slowly, cotton gold,
Secrets in their folds unfold.
Moonlight shines, a tale retold,
In the dark, we find the bold.

As night embraces, time suspends,
In twilight's glow, the spirit mends.
A canvas vast where magic blends,
Life's journey, where the heart transcends.

Beyond the Veil of Conscious Thought

In silent depths, where shadows play,
Thoughts unspool, they drift away.
Beyond the veil, in hues of gray,
Awakens truth in night's display.

Echoes linger in the mind,
Seeking solace, peace defined.
In quiet realms, the lost aligned,
Where every heartbeat is entwined.

Visions dance like fireflies' glow,
Fleeting whispers, soft and low.
In this space, we learn to grow,
Past the known, the depths we sow.

Across the chasm, dreams ignite,
In this boundless, starry night.
Past the veil, we find our light,
In the quiet, souls take flight.

Tapestry of Dreams Unraveled

Threads of night weave through my mind,
In every fold, a dream confined.
Colors swirl, a fate aligned,
In this tapestry, love is blind.

Memories stitched with golden thread,
Stories whispered, softly said.
Every tear, a path we tread,
In shadows cast, our hearts are led.

Images fade, yet still we strive,
In dreams alive, we learn to thrive.
In this dance, we dare to dive,
Unraveled dreams, where hopes revive.

A tapestry both rich and deep,
In every stitch, the secrets keep.
Through woven threads, our souls leap,
In slumber's arms, the heart shall reap.

The Secret of Endless Slumbers

In gentle night, where silence blooms,
The secret lies in quiet rooms.
Under stars, the soft heart grooms,
To drift away from worldly dooms.

Beneath the quilt of dreams untold,
Lies a warmth that breaks the cold.
In whispers of the night, we hold,
Together bound, our dreams unfold.

The essence of a peaceful sigh,
In fleeting moments, dreams will fly.
With every blink, we learn the why,
In endless slumbers, spirits high.

So close your eyes and breathe it in,
The secrets that the night begins.
In dreams, we dance, we lose, we win,
In endless slumbers, love's pure spin.

Visions Woven in Celestial Threads

In twilight's grasp, the stars align,
Whispers of dreams begin to twine.
Galaxies spin in a dance so bright,
Painting secrets across the night.

Threads of silver, soft and light,
Sketching stories in the flight.
Heaven's fabric, woven fine,
Stitching moments, yours and mine.

Softly glowing, moonbeams play,
Lacing shadows where shadows sway.
Each glimmer holds a tale long spun,
An echo of what's yet to come.

Gaze upon the skies so vast,
Feel the pull of the cosmic past.
In every twinkle, a promise said,
The visions woven in threads of red.

The Lattice of Nocturnal Whimsy

Beneath the stars, a net is laid,
Catching dreams that lightly fade.
A dance of shadows fills the air,
As whispers float without a care.

Incandescent flickers, dart and weave,
In tangled patterns, we believe.
A lattice formed of sighs and glee,
Cradles hopes like a lullaby's plea.

The night, adorned with playful charms,
Wraps the world in its arms.
Each twinkling light a spark so pure,
Embracing magic we all endure.

Through winding paths that softly bend,
The tapestry of dreams extends.
In this lattice, wild and free,
We find our hearts' sweet reverie.

Whirling Through the Night's Canvas

On midnight's brush, the colors flow,
Painting moments, soft and slow.
Strokes of darkness blend with light,
Creating worlds within the night.

Floating gently on the breeze,
Whispers twirl among the trees.
Each rustle tells a story grand,
Of dreams that glide, hand in hand.

Stars are dabs of golden hue,
Across the canvas, deep and true.
With every glance, a new design,
Whirling magic, intertwine.

In this realm where time stands still,
The heart beats to a painter's will.
Lost in the art, spirits soar,
Whirling through what we adore.

Forgotten Chronicles of the Night

Underneath the silver glow,
Lies the tales no one would know.
Whispered secrets, lost in time,
Echo softly, in rhythm and rhyme.

Each shadow holds a tale unclear,
Stories echo, drawing near.
Forgotten lore of ancient fright,
Breathes anew in the deep of night.

The moon casts light on pages worn,
Of heroes lost, and legends born.
In each flicker, truths reside,
Chronicles whispered by night's tide.

Listen close, and you shall find,
Treasures locked within the mind.
In the silence, history sings,
Forgotten dreams with fluttering wings.

Echoes of a Forgotten Realm

In whispers low, the shadows creep,
Through ancient woods where silence weeps.
Forgotten paths of tales once told,
In twilight's grasp, their secrets unfold.

A river flows where memories gleam,
Reflecting dreams, a fractured beam.
Beneath the boughs, a ghostly song,
Calls forth the lost, where they belong.

Time stands still in this hallowed space,
Each echo lingers, a soft embrace.
The wind caresses, a tender sigh,
Bidding farewell to days gone by.

In the fading light, we find our place,
In the heart of the realm, a sacred space.
With every breath, the past revives,
In echoes sweet, the spirit thrives.

The Pathway to Slumber's Secrets

In gentle dusk, the world grows dim,
A pathway leads where shadows swim.
Softly treading on velvet ground,
Whispers of dreams begin to sound.

Stars twinkle bright like hopes anew,
Guiding the heart with a tranquil hue.
Moonlight spills its silver grace,
As time drifts slowly in this place.

Beneath the boughs where silence reigns,
The heart unwinds, releasing pains.
Melodies of night weave through the air,
Cradling secrets meant to share.

Each step unveils a hidden truth,
Wrapped in the warmth of forgotten youth.
With every breath, let worries cease,
On slumber's path, we find our peace.

Silhouettes of Moonlit Fantasies

In dreams alight, the shadows play,
Moonlit figures lead the way.
Under stars, the night unfolds,
Whispers of magic, stories told.

Silhouettes dance upon the stream,
Brought to life from a distant dream.
Every glance, a spark ignites,
The heart takes flight on fanciful nights.

Through silver mist and twilight's glow,
Magic weaves in the softest flow.
In every corner, secrets dwell,
In moonlit fantasies, all is well.

Lost in wonder, we softly glide,
With every heartbeat, the worlds collide.
In shimmering hues, our spirits soar,
In the night's embrace, we seek for more.

Steps into an Enchanted Slumber

The hour draws near, a gentle sigh,
As dreams invite beneath the sky.
Each step we take, the world dissolves,
In the spell of night, our minds revolve.

Cradled in whispers of softest night,
The stars flicker with silver light.
Guiding us through a velvet haze,
Where magic dances in secret ways.

Embrace the calm, let worries slide,
In slumber's arms, we safely bide.
With heart unbound, we drift away,
Into the realms where shadows play.

With every breath, the night holds sway,
As dreams entwine in soft array.
In enchanted slumber, we shall find,
A world of wonder, a treasure blind.

Portals of Capture at Twilight's Gate

In shadows blend, the whispers sigh,
Opening doors where dreams comply.
The dusk unveils a hidden glance,
We step through time in fleeting dance.

Faded echoes of laughter sweet,
Carrying tales where hearts do meet.
Beneath the arch of fading light,
We grasp the night, prepare for flight.

Each moment held, a treasured pause,
Mysteries wrapped in gentle cause.
With eyes aflame, we chase the stars,
Designing futures from the scars.

The twilight calls, a siren's song,
We walk through paths where few belong.
In portals bright, our spirits dwell,
At twilight's gate, we weave our spell.

Tides of Imagination's Waters

Waves of thought like ebb and flow,
Carrying dreams where few may go.
In swirling depths, our visions rise,
Painting worlds beneath the skies.

The currents shift with whispered lore,
Unlocking tales from ocean's floor.
Each ripple holds a vibrant hue,
A canvas vast, forever new.

We sail on boats of fleeting time,
Embracing magic, rhythm, rhyme.
The tides will guide, both fierce and mild,
Imagination, forever wild.

As moonlit paths beckon us near,
We dive into the vibrant sphere.
In waters deep, we find our place,
In tides of thought, we dance with grace.

The Ascent of Wandering Spirits

Beneath the canopy of stars,
They rise above the world of scars.
In whispers soft, they seek the light,
Their journey marked by endless night.

Through valleys deep and mountains high,
They chase the dreams that never die.
With every breath, a story shared,
In echoes soft, their spirits bared.

They wander far, across the seas,
In silent winds, they find their ease.
Each heartbeat sings of places past,
The ascent grows, a spell is cast.

As dawn breaks through, their shadows fade,
Leaving behind the paths they made.
Yet in our hearts, they find their home,
In swirling skies where spirits roam.

Mosaics of the Night's Embrace

Stars like jewels across the sky,
Crafting tales as time goes by.
In twilight's grip, the dreams awake,
Where silence blooms and shadows break.

The night unfolds a canvas vast,
Each moment framed, each memory cast.
With every shimmer, stories weave,
In the embrace where hearts believe.

Colors dance in the softest sigh,
Reflections of the days gone by.
The darkness holds a sacred grace,
In every line, we find our place.

As dawn approaches, whispers fade,
Yet in our souls, the dreams are laid.
Mosaics shine, a bond unbroken,
In night's embrace, our hearts have spoken.

Transcending the Ordinary Slumber

In the hush of night, whispers collide,
Stars twinkle softly, secrets abide.
A journey begins on the silver tides,
Where shadows and dreams in silence reside.

Fleeting moments drift like autumn leaves,
Carrying hopes that the heart believes.
Beyond the veil where reality cleaves,
Awake in the night, the spirit weaves.

Colors of thought blend with the moon's glow,
Each pulse of the cosmos begins to flow.
Transcending the bounds of what we know,
In the embrace of night, we overflow.

As dawn approaches, dreams start to fade,
Yet their essence remains, unafraid.
Within the mind's eye, the journey stayed,
In the fabric of sleep, true life is laid.

The Essence of Dreams Revisited

In the quiet depth of the midnight hour,
Memory blooms like a fragrant flower.
Each petal holds whispers of hidden power,
A tapestry woven, sweet dreams empower.

Through corridors of the mind we glide,
Chasing reflections that can't abide.
With every heartbeat, worlds collide,
Unraveling mysteries that time can't hide.

Visions arise in the twilight glow,
Casting shadows where fantasies flow.
The essence of dreams, a river's slow,
Winding through realms where wonder will grow.

When morning breaks, and reality stirs,
The haunting of dreams still softly purrs.
In the gentle light, the spirit concurs,
To treasure the night, where true magic whirs.

Veils of Light and Shade

Tender whispers weave through the air,
Veils of light dance with shadows fair.
In the twilight's hush, secrets declare,
The realm where dreams linger without care.

Moonlight kisses the contours of night,
Illuminating paths and guiding light.
Beneath the surface, a world takes flight,
Intertwined in wonder, shy yet bright.

Each flicker reveals tales lost and found,
In the echoing silence, a gentle sound.
The essence of magic in each surround,
As we drift on currents of thought profound.

When dusk fades into dawn's embrace,
The veils lift gently, leaving no trace.
Yet the spirit of dreams, forever will grace,
The heart's quiet chamber, a timeless space.

Murmurs in the Realm of Sleep

Soft murmurs float through the velvet night,
In shadows that dance with whispers of light.
Nestled in dreams, emotions take flight,
Carried on breezes, a delicate sight.

Echoes of laughter from ages gone by,
Bathe the still air, like stars in the sky.
In the realm of sleep, where shadows lie,
Truths unravel softly, as moments sigh.

Threads of the past weave through time's embrace,
Each heartbeat a rhythm, a gentle grace.
In this sanctuary, we find our place,
Where dreams become memories, we interlace.

As dawn's fingers stretch and gently wake,
The whispers retreat, but their essence won't break.
In the realm of dreams, we find what we make,
With murmurs of night, our spirits awake.

Treading the Misty Edge of Dreams

In the dawn of whispering night,
Shadows dance in silver light.
Each step drenched in soft allure,
Hearts awaken, restless, sure.

Clouds like sails drift far above,
Carrying wishes weaved with love.
Floating on a gossamer thread,
Where hopes and visions gently tread.

Voices murmur, secrets shared,
In this realm, no hearts are spared.
Beneath the stars, time stands still,
Lost in magic, bound by will.

Dreams take flight on silent wings,
Embracing all the joy life brings.
We dare to chase the gleaming gleam,
Treading the misty edge of dream.

In the Garden of Fantastical Slumber

Beneath the boughs of ancient trees,
Whispers weave upon the breeze.
Petals fall with a silent grace,
Time unwinds in this sacred space.

Crickets sing an evening tune,
The moon smiles, a watchful rune.
Starlit paths invite the bold,
To wander where the dreams unfold.

Here, the flowers softly glow,
Carrying tales of long ago.
In this garden, spirits meet,
Every heartbeat feels complete.

Awake or lost in slumber's kiss,
All find treasures wrapped in bliss.
In dreams we plant our wildest schemes,
In the garden of fantastical dreams.

Tails from the Twilight Abyss

In shadows deep, where echoes fade,
Whispers of the night cascade.
Twilight creatures softly creep,
Guardians of the secrets they keep.

Fog rolls in, a thickened shroud,
Enveloping the world, profound.
Eyes that glimmer in distant haze,
Tell of ancient, haunted ways.

Dare we tread where few have walked?
In hushed tones, the night has talked.
Stories linger in the air,
Of those who lost their way, unaware.

With every shadow, a tail unfolds,
Adventures whispered in hues untold.
From darkest depths, we rise and see,
Tails from the twilight, wild and free.

Fleeing into Phantasmic Climes

When the sun dips low, we take flight,
Into the realms of dreams and night.
Chasing stars on a silver stream,
Fleeing deep into a waking dream.

Whirling colors in cosmic dance,
Holding tight to every chance.
In vibrant realms, our spirits soar,
Endless paths to explore and adore.

With every heartbeat, magic wakes,
Daring leaps that destiny makes.
We vanish in the twilight's gleam,
Lost in the folds of a phantasmic dream.

As dawn approaches, we feel the call,
But in our hearts, we've had it all.
Bound to the skies where dreams align,
Fleeing into phantasmic climes.

Whispers Beyond the Threshold

In twilight's glow, whispers sigh,
Secrets linger, softly nigh.
Footsteps dance on shadows cast,
A fleeting glimpse of dreams amassed.

Echoes murmur, lost in time,
Songs of heart, a gentle rhyme.
Voices call from realms unknown,
Inviting souls to paths they've sown.

Veils of Slumbering Realms

Beneath the moon's ethereal sheen,
Softly drift in blissful dream.
Veils of slumber cradle tight,
Whispered tales of ancient night.

In hushed embrace, shadows play,
Time dissolves, drifting away.
Stars awaken, twinkling bright,
Guiding souls through veils of light.

The Gateway to Enchanted Nights

Once upon a twilight breeze,
A gateway opens, hearts at ease.
Magic swirls in fragrant air,
Eager dreams beyond compare.

Flickering lights, a wondrous sight,
Stories spun from pure delight.
Each moment pulses, alive with grace,
A dance of joy in a sacred space.

Echoes of the Unseen Path

Echoes whisper through the trees,
Guiding hearts like a gentle breeze.
Unseen paths that twist and wind,
Lead to treasures yet to find.

Footprints lost in evening's mist,
Moments linger, sweetly kissed.
Trust the call of the unseen
For every shadow holds a dream.

Tunnels of Glimmering Thoughts

In tunnels deep where shadows play,
Glimmers dance in a gentle sway.
Whispers of dreams, secrets untold,
A journey through the mind unfolds.

Each thought a spark, a fleeting light,
Guiding souls through the endless night.
Echoes of laughter, echoes of pain,
In tunnels where visions remain.

The Labyrinth of Shimmering Visions

In the labyrinth, paths intertwine,
Shimmering visions, lost in time.
Every corner a story to find,
Mysteries hidden, fate intertwined.

A maze of colors, a dance of glow,
Leading hearts where dreams will flow.
Through curtains of twilight, softly we roam,
Guided by starlight, we find our home.

Climbing the Castles of Enchantment

Up the towers where hopes reside,
Castles glimmer, in dreams they abide.
Walls of wonder, stories untold,
In every stone, a treasure to hold.

Steps echoing with magical grace,
Climbing higher, the heart starts to race.
Through enchanted halls, where echoes blend,
Every moment, a tale without end.

The Archway of Mysterious Slumber

Beneath the archway, a world asleep,
Dreams like whispers, in shadows creep.
Mysterious tales of night and day,
In slumber's embrace, we gently sway.

Crossing the threshold, into the dark,
Where night blooms softly, just like a spark.
Each breath a secret, each sigh a song,
In the realm of slumber, we belong.